Lunar New Year

Around the World

A STUDIO PRESS BOOK

First published in the UK in 2022 by Studio Press Books,
an imprint of Bonnier Books UK,
4th Floor, Victoria House, Bloomsbury Square, London WC1B 4DA
Owned by Bonnier Books,
Sveavägen 56, Stockholm, Sweden

www.bonnierbooks.co.uk

Text © Amanda Li 2022
Illustrations © Angel Chang 2022

1 3 5 7 9 10 8 6 4 2

ISBN 978-1-80078-279-2

Edited by Emma Drage, Saaleh Patel and Frankie Jones
Designed by Rob Ward
Production by Emma Kidd

A CIP catalogue for this book is available from the British Library
Printed and bound in Poland

Lunar New Year

Around the World

Amanda Li

illustrated by

Angel Chang

STUDIO
PRESS

Hi, I'm Mei Lin and I'm from Beijing, China. I'm so excited because it's my favourite time of year — Lunar New Year!

All the shops and markets are busy with people buying food and decorations for their houses. We hang up red lanterns and red posters called couplets to wish everyone good luck for the year ahead.

Lunar New Year is also called
Spring Festival or Chinese New Year.
It is the biggest celebration of the year
for people in many East and South-East
Asian countries and communities
all over the world.

The colour red is everywhere at
Lunar New Year. In China, red is the
colour of happiness and good luck.

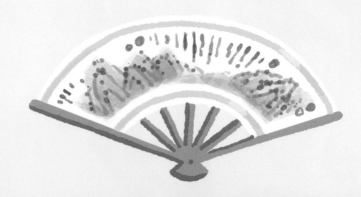

I'm Ryan and I live in Singapore. My aunties and uncles travel all the way from Canada to join us on Lunar New Year's Eve. They always give me a special red envelope, called *lai see*, as a gift. It has lucky money inside!

Everyone goes home for the celebrations if they can. Millions of people travel around the world at New Year. This is called *chunyun*.

Lunar New Year is celebrated in many different countries. The holiday always begins in January or February and lasts for fifteen days. The date changes every year depending on the first new moon.

I'm Emily, from Toronto, Canada. For Lunar New Year we share special dishes with different meanings. My favourite is long noodles, which means a long life. My grandmother says keep your plate full or your luck will run out!

Food is very important at Lunar New Year. People like to eat 'lucky' food. A whole fish means good luck and a healthy life.

Eating dumplings and spring rolls might make you rich in the New Year, while dried fruit and candies will make your life sweeter.

I'm Noah, in Sydney, Australia. I'm allowed to stay up and
watch the big firework display on Lunar New Year. It's so noisy!
The loud bangs are supposed to scare away monsters and bad luck.

Chinese legend says that a monster called Nian once terrified a village. A wise old man realised that Nian was scared of two things: the colour red and loud noises.

Everyone hung red lanterns on their houses and lit crackling bamboo. People still hang the lanterns but now they light fireworks to scare the monster away!

I'm Lamai, in Bangkok, Thailand.
At Lunar New Year, I go with my parents to
visit the local temples. We pray for good fortune
and give offerings of food and drink to our ancestors.
We also burn incense sticks and candles for them.

During Lunar New Year, people often pray
for past family members — their ancestors.
Sometimes they burn pretend paper money
in the streets to pass to their ancestors in
the afterlife. This is called 'ghost money'.

If the ancestors are happy, they might
send good luck your way for the New Year!

I'm Huang, from Taipei, Taiwan. I love the Lantern Festival at the end of the holiday. We write messages on lanterns and send them up into the sky. Seeing hundreds of glowing lanterns everywhere is amazing!

The Lantern Festival is the final
celebration of Lunar New Year.
When you let your lantern float away,
you are letting go of any worries.

The world's biggest Lantern Festival
is held in Taipei. It is a magical sight,
with huge paper lanterns shaped like
colourful animals and fun characters.

I'm Thuy and I live in Hanoi, Vietnam. *Tết* is our name for Lunar New Year.
I like going out to watch the street parades, especially the Lion Dance
and the Dragon Dance. The dragon's body moves up and down like
a rollercoaster – and sometimes smoke comes out of its mouth!

At Lunar New Year, different dances are performed for good luck.

For the Lion Dance, two dancers are inside the costume, moving together like a big cat.

For the Dragon Dance, at least nine performers hold poles to move the dragon's long body up and down.

I'm Arief, in Surakarta, Indonesia.
We call the holiday *Imlek* and we light lots of candles
in the temples. At our parade you can see thousands
of *kue keranjang* — tasty New Year cakes.
After the parade, we eat them all!

Every country has its own traditions at Lunar
New Year, although family, food and prayers
are important for everyone who celebrates it.

My name is Min-Joon and I live in Seoul, Korea, where Lunar New Year is called *Seollal.* We wear traditional clothes and eat rice cake soup with our families. Afterwards, children pay respect to their elders by bowing to them. They wish us luck and give us gifts of money.

I'm Jack and I live in London, England. Every year we get the Underground to Chinatown to eat Chinese food. In Trafalgar Square we watch the acrobats, the kung fu artists, the dances and, best of all, the fireworks!

There are Chinatowns all over the world where people come to celebrate Lunar New Year. New York, Vancouver, San Francisco, Melbourne and Bangkok all have famous Chinatowns – but there are many, many more.

I'm Riley, from the United States. Here in San Francisco, there is a huge Chinatown where the famous New Year Parade starts. At the end of the parade is an amazing Golden Dragon. It is 88 metres long and carried by 100 dancers!

I'm Aiden, in Hong Kong. Before Lunar New Year begins, everyone cleans their houses to sweep away bad luck. But once the holiday starts, nobody picks up a broom in case they sweep away the New Year good luck.

Lunar New Year has many traditions to do with luck:
- The third day of Lunar New Year is an unlucky day to have guests or visit friends.
- Red is a lucky colour, but nobody gives black or white gifts as these are unlucky.
- Nobody gives gifts of uneven numbers. Red envelope money should always be of an even number.

Sometimes we visit the Wishing Trees in Tai Po. We write our wish on paper and tie it to an orange. Then we throw the orange into the tree, and if it stays there, our wish will come true!

I'm Jamal, in New York. Did you know that every Lunar Year a different animal becomes the symbol for the new year?

You can find out which animal you are by the year you were born. I'm a Horse. Which animal are you?

The story goes that in ancient times, the Chinese Emperor wanted to find a way of measuring time. So he asked all the animals in the world to race across a river. The twelve animals who were the fastest were chosen as symbols for the Chinese Zodiac — one animal for each year.

MONKEY ROOSTER DOG GOAT PIG HORSE SNAKE DRAGON RABBIT TIGER OX RAT

猴 雞 狗 豬 鼠 牛 羊 兔 龍 蛇 馬 猴

2016 2017
2015 2004 2005 2018
2003 1992 1993 2006
1991 1994

2026 2019
2014 2008 2020
2002 1997 1995 2007
2025 1996
2013 2009
2001 2024 2010 2021
2023 2011 2022
2012 1999 1998
2000

KUNG HEI FAT CHOY!

HAPPY LUNAR NEW YEAR!

It's Mei Lin again! If you've never been to a Lunar New Year celebration before, make sure that you go one day. You will see fantastic parades, lanterns and fireworks and eat delicious food. You will have so much fun with your friends and family. And you can learn to say: *kung hei fat choy!*

Lunar New Year was first celebrated in China more than 3,000 years ago — but now it is celebrated all over the world! It is a wonderful way to say goodbye to the old year and welcome in the new.